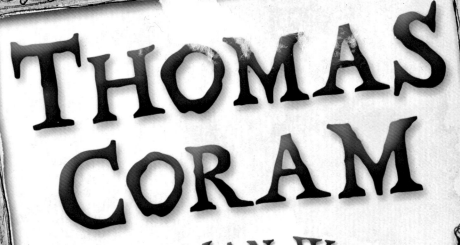

THOMAS CORAM

THE MAN WHO SAVED CHILDREN

By Harriet Amos & Alice Mayers

Illustrated by Jig

CONTENTS

★ You can find all underlined words in the glossary.

FACT All the artworks in this book can be seen in the Foundling Museum.

24324

THE STORY BEGINS

Let's go on a journey back in time.

Three hundred years ago London was a place where the rich enjoyed a fine and carefree life but the poor struggled to survive. Some people were so poor that they had no choice but to abandon their babies. This book tells how a man called Thomas Coram was determined to help these babies and build them a home, the <u>Foundling Hospital</u>.

My goodness! Who is looking after this baby? It will surely die all alone!

Captain Coram by Balthasar Nebot

FACT A <u>foundling</u> is a baby that has been abandoned by its parents and is discovered and cared for by other people.

? This is a painting of Thomas Coram. What do you think has happened to this baby?

INTRODUCTION TO THE PORTRAITS

**Many people played a part in the story of the <u>Foundling Hospital</u>.
Come and meet some of them. What do you think of their <u>portraits</u>?**

Hello, my name is Thomas Coram and this is my wife Eunice.

Thomas Coram by William Hogarth

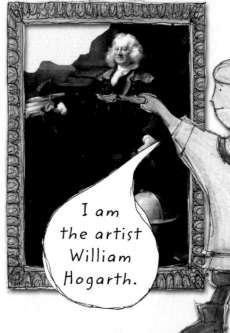

I am the artist William Hogarth.

Good day to you. I am Doctor Mead, <u>physician</u> to the King.

leech

I am George II, King of England.

My name is Japhet Hill. I live in the <u>Foundling Hospital</u>.

King George II by John Shackleton

4

Mrs Caroline Collingwood by the circle of John Downman

George Frideric Handel by Louis-François Roubiliac

Theodore Jacobsen by Thomas Hudson

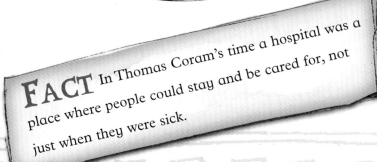

FACT In Thomas Coram's time a hospital was a place where people could stay and be cared for, not just when they were sick.

? What kind of people have their portraits painted and why?

THE YOUNG THOMAS CORAM

Let's find out more about our hero.

Thomas was born in England in 1668. He lived in Lyme Regis, Dorset. His father worked in the harbour.

Thomas found out at an early age what it meant to be lonely. His mother died when he was only four years old and his brother died as a baby.

FACT Death was common when Thomas was a boy. One baby in every five died before it was a year old, and half the <u>population</u> died before they reached 20 years old.

6

When Thomas was 11 years old he went to sea. He was sad to leave his friends and school but he loved the ocean life.

A Flagship Before the Wind Under Easy Sail, With a Cutter, a Ketch and Other Vessels by Charles Brooking

Are those English ships out there? I hope they are not pirates.

? Charles Brooking painted this picture to inspire boys to want to go to sea and become sailors. Would it inspire you?

When he was 16 he became an <u>apprentice</u> to a <u>shipwright</u> and learned how to build ships.

I must get these plans finished. Tomorrow we start building!

THE NEW WORLD

**When Thomas was 25 years old, he set sail for
America to build ships and seek his fortune.**

Unfortunately things did not
go quite to plan. Many
people in America did not
like Thomas and his ideas at
all. He ended up making lots
of enemies. . .

After 10 years in America, Thomas was tired of being bullied. He and his wife Eunice, who he had met and married in America, returned to England.

The March of the Guards to Finchley
by William Hogarth

THOMAS CORAM IN LONDON

Thomas lived in the East End of London. As he walked through the streets on his way to work he saw some terrible sights.

Thomas was horrified that so many babies and children lived and died on the streets. He couldn't understand why no one else seemed to care.

? Look at this <u>etching</u> called 'Gin Lane' by William Hogarth. How many signs of <u>poverty</u> can you see?

Gin Lane by William Hogarth

Thomas had an idea. He would build a safe home for children, where they would be looked after, with clean clothes to wear, fresh food to eat, doctors to keep them healthy and teachers to show them how to read and write.

I will build a home for these children. It will be called the <u>Foundling Hospital</u>.

FACT In the 1700s more than 1,000 babies were abandoned on the streets of London every year.

What a noble idea, but will the King agree?

? This picture shows the home that was eventually built for the <u>foundlings</u>. Does it look like a good place for babies and children to live? Would you like to live here?

Front of the Foundling Hospital

THOMAS CORAM'S 17-YEAR CAMPAIGN

Before Thomas could build the <u>Foundling Hospital</u> he needed the King's permission, a signed and sealed <u>Royal Charter</u>.

1722 Thomas went to see the King.

> The King hasn't got time to see the likes of you.

It was far harder than he had expected. The King did not think poor children were important. Thomas, however, was determined and he came up with a plan. He decided he would ask all the rich and important men to sign a <u>petition</u> to take to the King. Then the King would have to listen! Unfortunately, the gentlemen did not care either.

12

1729 The Duchess of Somerset signed the petition.

So Thomas asked the gentlemen's wives.

And then everyone wanted to sign.

1739 On 17 October 1739, after 17 years of campaigning, when Thomas had a total of 375 signatures, including 21 Ladies, 25 Dukes, 31 Earls, 38 Knights, one Bishop and the Prime Minister, the King finally gave the Foundling Hospital the Royal Charter.

BUILDING THE HOSPITAL

With the <u>Royal Charter</u> in hand the real work could now begin.

On 20 November 1739 Thomas presented the Charter to a grand audience. It was a great occasion. Thomas realised there were many people who shared his dream and who wanted to help build the hospital.

The Royal Charter

I now present His Majesty's <u>Royal Charter</u> for establishing a Hospital for abandoned children.

Where on earth are we going to build it?

This is such a wonderful idea!

How can we raise all the money?

Thomas and his friends William Hogarth, Dr Mead, Theodore Jacobsen and George Frideric Handel came up with some plans . . .

I, the King's <u>physician</u>, will keep the children healthy.

I am going to hold a concert! That will raise lots of money.

I've found the perfect place to build our Hospital, come and see.

And I'll decorate the walls with my pictures. All the rich people will come to see them and give money to the Hospital.

FACT When the <u>Foundling Hospital</u> opened it was surrounded by fields. Since then London has grown around it.

? Look at the clothes and objects in these <u>portraits</u>. What do they tell you about these men?

THE BABIES ARRIVE

In 1741 the <u>Foundling Hospital</u> finally opened and mothers queued at the doors hoping to leave their babies.

FACT

The <u>Foundling Hospital</u> is quite a strange name. The babies were not really <u>foundlings</u>, they were babies whose mothers and fathers could not look after them.

Remember, you are my <u>servant</u>! If you want to keep your job and a roof over your head you will have to get rid of that baby.

From then on, poor and tearful mothers handed over their babies. They hoped that at the <u>Foundling Hospital</u> their babies would survive.

FACT Mothers left a <u>token</u>, with their baby. For example, a necklace. They were also given a receipt in case they should ever reclaim their child.

Peasant Boy by John Singleton Copley

A Roaring Success

Feeding and caring for the children was expensive but Handel and Hogarth's brilliant ideas helped raise lots of money.

Paintings
from left to right

Moses brought before Pharaoh's Daughter by William Hogarth

A View of the Foundling Hospital from the Fields by Richard Wilson

A View of the Charterhouse from the Terrace by Thomas Gainsborough

? Do you know the story of Moses? Why do you think Hogarth chose to paint Moses for the Foundling Hospital?

Lovely paintings.

Let's go and hear the foundlings sing!

Hogarth and his friends decorated rooms with paintings and sculptures. Wealthy ladies and gentlemen flocked to visit and the Foundling Hospital became England's first public art gallery. The visitors were impressed and gave generously.

Handel performed concerts in the <u>Foundling Hospital</u> chapel. The chapel was small and lots of people wanted to attend, so the ladies were asked not to wear bulky hoops under their skirts and gentlemen had to leave their cumbersome swords at home. The concerts were a great success.

The Foundling Hospital: the Chapel by John Sanders

FACT For entertainment, on a Sunday afternoon the rich liked to go and watch the lions in the Tower of London, the mad people in <u>Bedlam</u> or the <u>foundlings</u> in the <u>Foundling Hospital</u> eating their lunch!

THOMAS CORAM'S LAST DAYS

As an old man, Thomas was often seen in the grounds of the <u>Foundling Hospital</u>, handing out treats of gingerbread to the children.

Yummy, Gingerbread! It was lumpy gruel for breakfast.

Thomas died when he was 83 years old. The <u>Foundling Hospital</u> governors gave him a grand funeral. Many Lords and Ladies attended but most important of all, the <u>foundlings</u> went too.

In his old age Thomas was very poor. He had spent so much time and money helping others that he had little left over for himself.

Mr Coram's here!

FACT 27,000 children grew up in the <u>Foundling Hospital</u> until it closed in 1953.

23

The Foundling Hospital Photo Album

For over 200 years the <u>Foundling Hospital</u> carried on Thomas's work caring for children.

Girls in their playroom.

Girls exercising.

The Foundling Hospital flag.

Girls and boys singing.

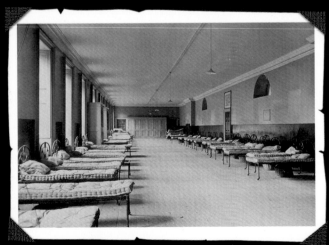
One of the wards.

FACT Until they were five years old, the <u>foundlings</u> lived with a foster mother in the countryside.

Ring - a- ring o' roses.

Boys learning to read.

Summer camp.

Clowns visiting the Foundling Hospital.

Queuing for Spotted Dick!

The Duke of Connaught on a visit.

THOMAS CORAM TODAY

The Foundling Hospital closed in 1953 but the charity Coram Family continues to look after children. The Foundling Museum reminds us of the good work of Thomas Coram, William Hogarth and George Frideric Handel. Coram's Fields is a place where children can play safely.

Today there are lots of people to help children and laws to protect them.

Despite all these changes many children are not getting the care that they need.

DID YOU KNOW?

The site of the <u>Foundling Hospital</u> was sold to Coram's Fields to be made into a children's playground. It is very special, as adults are allowed in only if they are accompanied by a child.

Firefighters save us from danger.

Police officers keep us safe.

Nurses keep us healthy.

Coram Family looks after children, young people and also their families.

 Coram Family helps children who cannot live with their parents, sometimes finding new parents to look after them.

 Coram Family helps children and teenagers to get on well with others and deal with bullies.

 Coram Family helps children keep in touch with their parents if they are unable to live with them.

 Coram Family helps parents look after their children.

FOUNDLING INVESTIGATION

Do you remember Japhet Hill?

Now meet Jasmine Hill his great great great great great grand daughter. Jasmine has come to the Foundling Museum to find out more about Japhet. She knows that he was left at the <u>Foundling Hospital</u> as a baby a very long time ago.

Name of the Child.....	No	Date of Arrival	Business of Master	Date of Apprenticeship
Japhet Hill	8254	April 26 1756	Clockmaker	May 4 1768
Thomas Kent	8942	October 11 1756	Farmer	April 25 1768

Look I have found him: Japhet Hill, <u>foundling number 8254</u>. You can see the date he arrived at the <u>Foundling Hospital</u> and what happened to him when he left.

Here he is again in the register for the infirmary.

Name · Disease

Japhet Hill · Sore mouth

Ralph Brent · Stone in His Bladder

This is a list of everything Japhet was wearing the day his mum left him at the Foundling Hospital.

8234 · April 26 1756

Marks and Cloathing of the Child

Cap
Forehead-Cloth
Frock
Petticoat
Robe
Sleeves
Blanket
Shirt
Stockings

Marks on the Body

Blue Necklace

A Boy Christened

? How old was Japhet when he left the Hospital, and what did he go on to do?

? Can you spot any old English spelling on this page?

Oh, his mother also left a blue necklace, I bet that is his token.

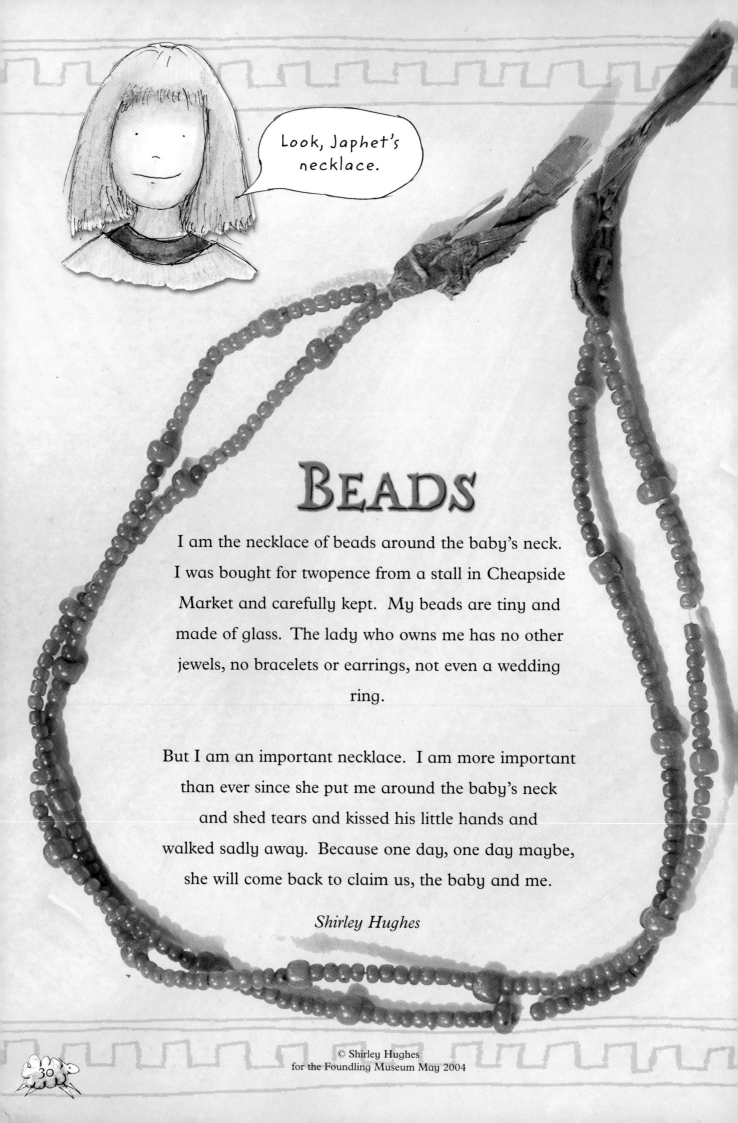

Look, Japhet's necklace.

BEADS

I am the necklace of beads around the baby's neck.
I was bought for twopence from a stall in Cheapside
Market and carefully kept. My beads are tiny and
made of glass. The lady who owns me has no other
jewels, no bracelets or earrings, not even a wedding
ring.

But I am an important necklace. I am more important
than ever since she put me around the baby's neck
and shed tears and kissed his little hands and
walked sadly away. Because one day, one day maybe,
she will come back to claim us, the baby and me.

Shirley Hughes

GLOSSARY

<u>Anglican;</u> a type of Christian

<u>Apprentice;</u> a person who is learning a trade from an expert

<u>Architecture;</u> the design of buildings

<u>Bedlam;</u> in Thomas's day, this was a hospital where people suffering from mental illness lived

<u>Bible;</u> sacred and important writings of the Jewish and Christian religions

<u>Composer;</u> a person who writes music

<u>Etching;</u> a special kind of printing

<u>Foundling;</u> a baby who has been abandoned by its parents and is discovered and cared for by other people

<u>Foundling Hospital;</u> the home for babies and children set up by Thomas Coram

<u>Infirmary;</u> a small hospital or sick room

<u>Petition;</u> a formal written request often signed by many people

<u>Population;</u> all the people who live in one place

<u>Portrait;</u> a picture or a model of a person

<u>Poverty;</u> having very little money or possessions

<u>Puritan;</u> a type of Christian who lives by very strict religious principles

<u>Physician;</u> another word for a doctor

<u>Royal Charter;</u> written permission from the King or Queen

<u>Servant;</u> a person employed to perform domestic chores

<u>Shipwright;</u> someone who builds ships

<u>Spotted Dick;</u> a pudding made with currants

<u>Token;</u> a thing that is important to its owner, like a keepsake. They were left with babies to prove who was their mother or father

PEOPLE INDEX

First published in Great Britain by the Foundling Museum 2006

Text and design © The Foundling Museum 2006
Beads © Shirley Hughes 2004
Illustrations © James Alistair Cochrane 2006
www.jigartsworkshops.com

The illustrator has asserted his moral rights.

ISBN 0-9551808-0-5

1 3 5 7 9 10 8 6 4 2

Design by Mandy Norman
Printed by BAS Printers, Salisbury, Wiltshire

The Foundling Museum
40 Brunswick Square
London
WC1N 1AZ

Telephone: 020 7841 3600

www.foundlingmuseum.org.uk